YOUR FREE GIFT !!

As a token of my thanks for taking out time to read my book, I would like to offer you a **Free-Gift**:

Click the Below Link and Download your **Free eBook PDF**.

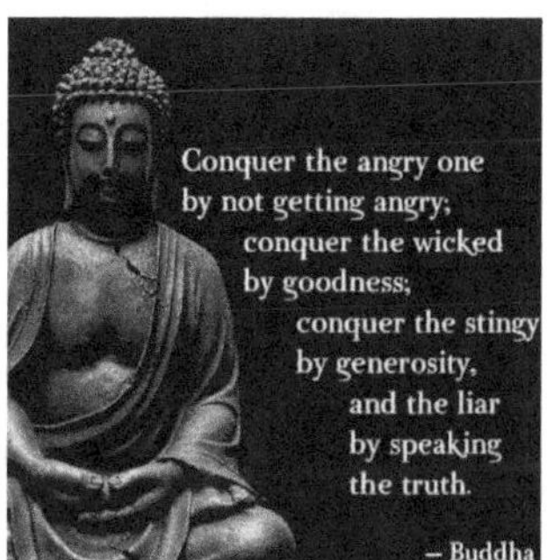

"The Power of Community: Thriving To

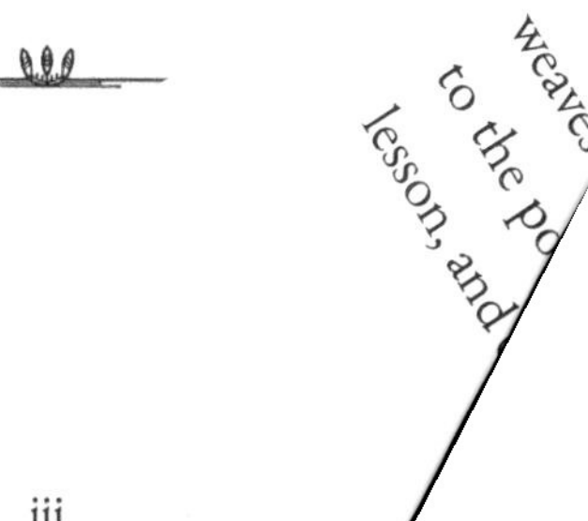

ABOUT THE AUTHOR

Prem Sagar Sunchu, the Accomplished Author of "The Stress Detox"

M eet Mr. Prem Sagar, an ordinary soul born in the vibrant city of Secunderabad, India, where the tapestry of life stories of resilience and dreams. His journey is a testament wer of perpetual learning, where every encounter is a every moment holds the potential for growth.

THE STRESS DETOX

Cultivate Inner Calm, Elevate Energy Levels, Enhance Emotional Stability, and Conquer Stress for Lifelong Happiness

PREM SAGAR SUNCHU

Copyright © 2024 by Prem Sagar Sunchu

All rights reserved.

No part of this book may be reproduced in any form without permission in writing from the author.

No part of this publication may be reproduced or transmitted in any form or by any means, mechanical or electronic, including photocopying or recording, or by any information storage and retrieval system, or transmitted by email or by any other means whatsoever without permission in writing from the author.

A man of many dimensions, Mr. Sagar embodies the qualities of a perpetual student, a dedicated listener, and a dreamer who gazes at the stars but keeps his feet firmly grounded. His aspirations soar high, and his relentless pursuit of them is fueled by a genuine desire to make a positive impact on those around him.

Having served as a Chief Manager in the prestigious State Bank of India, Mr. Sagar brings a wealth of experience from the world of banking. However, for him, retirement isn't a conclusion but a commencement—a reminder that life's true journey begins when one can reflect on the wisdom gained from the first innings.

In Mr. Sagar's view, retirement is not a retreat but a stepping stone to a realm of infinite possibilities. It's an opportunity to surpass the ordinary, where the canvas of life awaits new brushstrokes of creativity and purpose. For him, the "be good and do good policy" isn't just a mantra; it's a guiding principle that shapes his approach to life.

As he embraces the second innings, Mr. Sagar encourages others to view retirement not as a winding down but as a springboard to new endeavors. It's a time when accumulated wisdom meets fresh energy, and the monotony of routine gives way to the vibrancy of creativity. His belief is clear: retirement is not just a number; it's a chapter where the richness of experience meets the possibilities in abundance.

In the world of Mr. Prem Sagar, retirement is not a period of rest but a canvas waiting to be painted with the colors of newfound wisdom, creativity, and a different outlook on life.

Prem Sagar Sunchu

M.Com, LLM, Certified Independent Director (IICA) GOI, Author, Sole Arbitrator and Legal Consultant, Freelancer

ACKNOWLEDGEMENTS

In profound gratitude, I extend heartfelt appreciation to my amazing parents. To my caring and resilient mother, **Smt. S.L. Lakshmi**, who gracefully navigated the challenges of my father's service transfers, made countless sacrifices to bind our family together. My father, **Shri S.R. Lakshman Rao**, stands as my enduring role model—his post-retirement vibrancy, marked by a dedicated hobby of reading and writing, serves as the very foundation that propels me into the realm of authorship.

A debt of gratitude is owed to my beautiful wife, **Smt. S.P. Padma Sree** is a constant source of inspiration, unwavering strength, and invaluable guidance. Balancing family responsibilities and the intricate path of an author, her presence has been the foundation of my journey.

To my handsome sons, **S.P. Gautam Sagar, S.P. Prayag Sagar, and S.P. Akshaj Sagar**, whose unwavering support and responsibility bear testament to the great strength they provide. Their motivation fuels my endeavors across all the diverse traits I undertake.

I owe thanks to **Mr. Som Bathla**, an **Amazon #1 Bestselling** author, for his mentorship, motivation, and guidance in the realms of **Writing, Self-Publishing, and Launching Books**. His support has been instrumental in initiating my journey as an Authorpreneur.

My Sincere thanks to **Mr. Sooraj Achar**, who is also an Amazon Bestselling Author, for his **Professional Editing,** Formatting, and Publishing support.

In acknowledging these pillars of support, I am reminded that the tapestry of my life and authorial pursuit is woven with threads of love, sacrifice, and inspiration. With profound thanks to my family, who stand as my bedrock of strength and motivation.

DEDICATION

To the guiding stars of my universe—my Parents, Grandparents, Parents-in-law, Brothers, Sisters, the cherished members of our extended Family and Friends. Their unwavering support and boundless encouragement have been the driving force behind my Author Journey.

In the tapestry of my life, each of them has woven threads of inspiration and resilience, transforming mere words into stories and dreams into realities. Their confidence in me has been a constant source of strength, propelling me forward through the path of this journey.

With heartfelt gratitude, I dedicate the pages of my work to the pillars of love and encouragement that they are, recognizing that every word I pen is a tribute to the collective spirit of our family. May this dedication reflect the depth of my appreciation for the profound impact they have had on my creative journey.

"The Stress Detox" is my first book in the series of five books-**"The Resilient Mind."**

CONTENTS

INTRODUCTION

In our fast-paced, ever-evolving world, stress has become an almost inevitable companion. Whether it's work-related pressures, personal challenges, or the relentless influx of information and demands from daily life, stress infiltrates our lives in myriad ways. Yet, while stress is a natural response to life's pressures, it doesn't have to dominate or diminish our quality of life. This book, "The Stress Detox," is your comprehensive guide to understanding, managing, and ultimately mastering stress.

Stress is not just a fleeting inconvenience; it's a pervasive issue that impacts our physical health, emotional well-being, and overall happiness. Chronic stress can lead to a host of problems, including anxiety, depression, sleep disturbances, and even serious health conditions like heart disease and hypertension. However, by cultivating inner calm, elevating our energy levels, enhancing emotional stability, and adopting effective strategies, we can conquer stress and pave the way for lifelong happiness.

Understanding Stress

The first step in mastering stress is understanding it. In the opening chapter, we will delve into the nature of stress, exploring its physiological and psychological aspects. We'll examine how stress manifests in the body and mind, the different types of stress (acute, episodic, and chronic), and the common triggers that set off our stress response. By understanding the root causes and effects of stress, we lay the foundation for effective management.

Mindset and Attitude

Our mindset and attitude play crucial roles in how we perceive and handle stress. Chapter Two focuses on developing a resilient mindset and fostering positive attitudes that help us navigate stressful situations with grace and composure. We will explore techniques for cultivating optimism, practicing gratitude, and embracing a growth mindset, all of which contribute to a healthier, more balanced perspective on life.

Physical Strategies for Stress Management

Our physical well-being is intricately connected to our stress levels. In Chapter Three, we will explore a range of physical strategies to manage and reduce stress. From exercise and nutrition to relaxation techniques like yoga and meditation, this chapter provides practical tools to strengthen our bodies and calm our minds. These strategies not only help in the immediate relief of stress but also build long-term resilience.

Emotional and Social Strategies

Humans are social beings, and our emotional and social lives significantly influence our stress levels. Chapter Four delves into emotional intelligence, effective communication, and the importance of social support. We will discuss how to manage our emotions, build and maintain supportive relationships, and seek help when needed. By fostering strong emotional and social connections, we create a robust support system that buffers us against stress.

Time Management and Productivity

One of the most common sources of stress is the feeling of being overwhelmed by too many tasks and too little time. Chapter Five offers strategies for effective time management and productivity. We will explore techniques such as prioritization, delegation, and the use of tools and systems to organize our lives. By mastering time management, we can reduce stress and increase our efficiency and satisfaction in both personal and professional spheres.

Long-Term Strategies for Stress Mastery

Finally, Chapter Six focuses on long-term strategies for mastering stress. This chapter emphasizes the importance of sustainable practices that integrate stress management into our daily lives. We will discuss habits, routines, and lifestyle changes that promote enduring calm and resilience. By committing to these long-term strategies, we can achieve a state of stress mastery that supports lifelong happiness and well-being.

A Journey to Lifelong Happiness

Embarking on "The Stress Detox" journey means committing to a transformative process that not only addresses immediate stressors but also builds a resilient, happier, and healthier you. Each chapter of this book is designed to equip you with the knowledge, tools, and strategies needed to cultivate inner calm, elevate your energy levels, enhance emotional stability, and conquer stress. Together, let's embark on this journey to lifelong happiness, one step at a time.

CHAPTER 1

UNDERSTANDING STRESS

"Stress is not what happens to us. It's our response to what happens. And response is something we can choose." — Maureen Killoran

Introduction

Stress is an inevitable part of life that can affect everyone, regardless of age, occupation, or lifestyle. While often viewed negatively, stress can also have positive aspects, motivating us to achieve goals and meet deadlines. Understanding stress in its various forms is crucial for managing its impact on our well-being. This chapter delves into the definition and types of stress, explores its physiological effects, identifies common stressors in modern life, and provides self-assessment tools to gauge personal stress levels and triggers.

Introduction to Stress: Definition and Types of Stress

Definition of Stress: Stress is the body's response to any demand or challenge, whether physical, emotional, or mental. It is a natural reaction designed to help individuals cope with threats and pressures, often referred to as the "fight-or-flight" response.

Types of Stress

1. **Acute Stress:** This is short-term stress that arises from specific events or situations. It can be positive or negative, such as preparing for a presentation or experiencing a minor car accident. Acute stress is usually intense but brief and can sometimes be beneficial by enhancing focus and energy levels.

2. **Chronic Stress:** Unlike acute stress, chronic stress persists over an extended period. It often results from ongoing situations such as financial problems, relationship issues, or a demanding job. Chronic stress can be detrimental to health, leading to serious physical and mental health issues if not managed properly.

3. **Eustress:** This is a positive stress that energizes and mo-

tivates individuals. Eustress is associated with feelings of excitement and fulfillment, such as starting a new job, getting married, or engaging in a favorite hobby. It helps enhance performance and well-being when experienced in moderation.

The Physiology of Stress

Stress triggers a cascade of physiological responses designed to prepare the body for immediate action. Understanding these responses can help us recognize the signs of stress and take steps to manage it effectively.

How Stress Affects the Body and Mind

1. **The Nervous System:** When faced with a stressful situation, the brain activates the autonomic nervous system (ANS), which consists of the sympathetic and parasympathetic nervous systems. The sympathetic nervous system (SNS) triggers the "fight-or-flight" response, releasing adrenaline and cortisol. These hormones increase heart rate, blood pressure, and energy supplies, preparing the body to respond to the perceived threat.

2. **The Endocrine System:** The hypothalamus-pituitary-adrenal (HPA) axis is a major part of the endocrine system involved in the stress response. The hypothalamus signals the pituitary gland to release adrenocorticotropic

hormone (ACTH), which then stimulates the adrenal glands to produce cortisol. Cortisol helps maintain fluid balance and blood pressure, and it regulates functions that are not crucial in a fight-or-flight situation, such as digestion and growth.

3. **The Immune System:** Short-term stress can boost the immune system by preparing the body to heal from injuries. However, chronic stress suppresses immune function, making individuals more susceptible to infections and illnesses.

4. **The Musculoskeletal System:** Stress causes muscles to tense up as a way of protecting against injury. Chronic stress can lead to muscle tension, headaches, and other musculoskeletal problems.

5. **The Respiratory and Cardiovascular Systems:** Stress can cause rapid breathing (hyperventilation) and increase heart rate, potentially leading to panic attacks. Long-term stress contributes to hypertension, heart disease, and other cardiovascular issues.

6. **The Digestive System:** Stress affects the digestive system by altering appetite, causing nausea, and potentially leading to conditions like irritable bowel syndrome (IBS) and acid reflux.

Identifying Stressors

Understanding common sources of stress can help individuals pinpoint their own stressors and develop strategies to manage them.

Common Sources of Stress in Modern Life

1. **Work-Related Stress:** Job demands, tight deadlines, lack of control, and workplace conflicts are significant sources of stress. The pressure to perform and achieve can lead to burnout if not managed effectively.

2. **Financial Stress:** Concerns about money, debt, and financial stability can cause significant stress. Managing expenses, saving for the future, and dealing with unexpected costs are common financial stressors.

3. **Relationship Stress:** Interpersonal relationships, whether with family, friends, or colleagues, can be a source of stress. Miscommunication, conflicts, and lack of support can strain relationships and contribute to stress.

4. **Health-Related Stress:** Chronic illnesses, injuries, and concerns about one's health or the health of loved ones can be stressful. Managing medical conditions and navigating the healthcare system are common health-related stressors.

5. **Major Life Changes:** Events such as moving, changing jobs, getting married, or experiencing a loss can disrupt normal routines and cause stress. Even positive changes can be stressful, as they require adjustment and adaptation.

6. **Environmental Stress:** Noise, pollution, overcrowding, and living in unsafe neighborhoods can contribute to stress. Environmental stressors are often beyond an individual's control, making them particularly challenging to manage.

7. **Daily Hassles:** Minor irritations and inconveniences, such as traffic jams, long lines, and technology issues, can accumulate and contribute to overall stress levels.

Self-Assessment

Recognizing personal stress levels and triggers is the first step toward managing stress effectively. Self-assessment tools and techniques can help individuals gain insight into their stressors and responses.

Tools and Techniques to Identify Personal Stress Levels and Triggers

1. **Stress Diaries:** Keeping a stress diary involves recording stressful events, the physical and emotional responses to

them, and any coping strategies used. Reviewing the diary can help identify patterns and common stressors.

2. **Self-Assessment Questionnaires:** Various self-assessment questionnaires, such as the Perceived Stress Scale (PSS) and the Stress Symptom Checklist, can help measure stress levels and identify specific stressors.

3. **Mindfulness and Self-Reflection:** Practicing mindfulness and self-reflection involves paying attention to thoughts, feelings, and physical sensations without judgment. This can help individuals become more aware of their stress triggers and responses.

4. **Body Scans:** A body scan is a mindfulness technique that involves focusing attention on different parts of the body to identify areas of tension and stress. This can help individuals become more attuned to their physical stress responses.

5. **Physiological Measures:** Monitoring physiological indicators such as heart rate, blood pressure, and cortisol levels can provide objective measures of stress. Wearable devices and biofeedback tools can help track these indicators over time.

6. **Journaling:** Writing about thoughts and feelings related to stress can provide insight into personal stressors and coping mechanisms. Journaling can also serve as a ther-

apeutic outlet for processing emotions.

Conclusion

Understanding stress, its physiological effects, and its common sources is essential for managing it effectively. By identifying personal stress levels and triggers through self-assessment tools and techniques, individuals can develop strategies to mitigate stress and enhance their well-being. In the following chapters, we will explore various approaches and techniques to manage and reduce stress, empowering you to lead a healthier, more balanced life.

Resources

1. **Books:**

   - "Why Zebras Don't Get Ulcers" by Robert M. Sapolsky

   - "The Relaxation and Stress Reduction Workbook" by Martha Davis, Elizabeth Robbins Eshelman, and Matthew McKay

   - "The Stress Solution" by Rangan Chatterjee

2. **Websites:**

   - American Psychological Association (www.apa.org)

- Stress Management Society (www.stress.org.uk)

- Mayo Clinic Stress Management (www.mayoclinic.org)

3. **Apps:**

- Headspace (mindfulness and meditation)

- Calm (meditation and relaxation)

- MyLife (personalized mindfulness)

4. **Articles:**

- "Stress and Health: Psychological, Behavioral, and Biological Determinants" (Annual Review of Clinical Psychology)

- "The Effects of Stress on Your Body" (Healthline)

By gaining a comprehensive understanding of stress and its impact, you can begin to take proactive steps towards managing it and improving your overall quality of life.

Chapter 2

MINDSET AND ATTITUDE

"Whether you think you can, or you think you can't –
you're right." — Henry Ford

Introduction

Our mindset and attitude towards life play a crucial role in how we perceive and manage stress. By cultivating a positive mindset and developing mental resilience, we can transform our approach to stress, viewing challenges as opportunities for growth rather than obstacles. This chapter explores the power of perspective, techniques to build resilience, the importance of positive thinking, and practices like gratitude and mindfulness to shift focus and reduce stress.

The Power of Perspective: How Mindset Influences Stress Perception

Understanding Mindset

Mindset refers to the established set of attitudes held by an individual. Psychologist Carol Dweck's research highlights two primary types of mindset: fixed and growth. A fixed mindset assumes that abilities and intelligence are static and cannot be changed, leading to a tendency to avoid challenges and view failure as a reflection of one's inherent limitations. In contrast, a growth mindset embraces challenges, persists in the face of setbacks, and views effort as a path to mastery.

Mindset and Stress Perception

The way we perceive stress is significantly influenced by our mindset. Individuals with a fixed mindset are more likely to feel overwhelmed by stress, viewing it as a threat that they are powerless to overcome. On the other hand, those with a growth mindset see stress as a natural part of the learning process and an opportunity to develop new skills and resilience.

Changing Your Perspective

Adopting a growth mindset involves recognizing that we have the power to change our responses to stress. By reframing stressful situations as opportunities for growth, we can reduce the negative impact of stress on our well-being. Techniques such as cognitive restructuring, which involves challenging and changing negative thought patterns, can help shift our perspective and improve our stress response.

Developing Resilience: Building Mental Toughness to Handle Stress

What is Resilience?

Resilience is the capacity to recover quickly from difficulties and adapt well in the face of adversity, trauma, or significant sources of stress. It involves maintaining flexibility and balance in life as we deal with stressful circumstances and traumatic events.

Building Resilience

1. **Cultivate a Strong Support Network:** Having a network of supportive relationships can provide a buffer against stress. Friends, family, and colleagues can offer emotional support, practical assistance, and different perspectives on challenges.

2. **Develop Problem-Solving Skills:** Being able to approach problems with a clear and strategic mindset is crucial for resilience. Breaking down problems into man-

ageable parts and developing actionable plans can reduce feelings of overwhelm.

3. **Embrace Change:** Accepting that change is a part of life can help build resilience. Flexibility and adaptability allow us to navigate life's uncertainties more effectively.

4. **Practice Self-Care:** Taking care of our physical, emotional, and mental health is fundamental to resilience. Regular exercise, healthy eating, sufficient sleep, and relaxation techniques can strengthen our ability to handle stress.

5. **Set Goals:** Having clear, achievable goals can provide direction and purpose. Working towards these goals, even in small steps, can build confidence and resilience.

Positive Thinking: Techniques to Cultivate a Positive Outlook

The Power of Positive Thinking

Positive thinking involves focusing on the good in any given situation. It doesn't mean ignoring reality or challenges but rather approaching them with a constructive and optimistic attitude. Positive thinking has been linked to numerous benefits, including reduced stress levels, better psychological and physical well-being, and improved coping skills during stressful situations.

Techniques to Cultivate Positive Thinking

1. **Affirmations:** Repeating positive statements about oneself can help shift mindset. Affirmations like "I am capable," "I am resilient," and "I can handle challenges" reinforce a positive self-image and mindset.

2. **Visualization:** Imagining positive outcomes and scenarios can help reduce anxiety and stress. Visualization techniques can be particularly useful in preparing for stressful events or situations.

3. **Positive Journaling:** Writing about positive experiences and things you are grateful for can enhance positive thinking. Keeping a gratitude journal, where you list things you are thankful for each day, can shift focus from negative to positive aspects of life.

4. **Surround Yourself with Positivity:** Engaging with positive people, content, and environments can reinforce positive thinking. Avoiding negative influences and media can help maintain an optimistic outlook.

5. **Challenge Negative Thoughts:** Whenever a negative thought arises, challenge its validity and replace it with a positive or more balanced thought. This practice, known as cognitive restructuring, can gradually change thought patterns and attitudes.

Gratitude and Mindfulness: Practices to Shift Focus and Reduce Stress

The Role of Gratitude

Gratitude involves recognizing and appreciating the positive aspects of life. Research shows that practicing gratitude can significantly improve mental health, increase happiness, and reduce stress. Gratitude helps shift focus from what is lacking to what is abundant, fostering a sense of contentment and well-being.

Practices to Cultivate Gratitude

1. **Gratitude Journaling:** Regularly writing down things you are grateful for can enhance feelings of gratitude. Reflecting on these entries during challenging times can provide perspective and comfort.

2. **Gratitude Letters:** Writing letters of thanks to people who have had a positive impact on your life can deepen feelings of gratitude and strengthen relationships.

3. **Daily Gratitude Rituals:** Incorporating simple gratitude practices into daily routines, such as expressing thanks before meals or at bedtime, can help maintain a grateful mindset.

The Role of Mindfulness

Mindfulness involves paying full attention to the present moment without judgment. It can help reduce stress by increasing awareness of thoughts, feelings, and bodily sensations, allowing individuals to respond to stressors more effectively rather than reacting impulsively.

Practices to Cultivate Mindfulness

1. **Mindful Breathing:** Focusing on the breath is a simple yet powerful mindfulness practice. Paying attention to each inhale and exhale can calm the mind and reduce stress.

2. **Body Scan Meditation:** This involves paying attention to different parts of the body, noting any sensations, tensions, or discomfort. This practice can increase body awareness and promote relaxation.

3. **Mindful Observation:** Taking a few moments to observe and appreciate the environment, such as noticing the colors of a flower or the sound of birds, can help ground you in the present moment.

4. **Mindful Movement:** Activities like yoga, tai chi, or walking can be practiced mindfully by focusing on the movements and sensations of the body.

Conclusion

Our mindset and attitude are powerful tools in managing stress. By understanding the influence of perspective, developing resilience, cultivating positive thinking, and practicing gratitude and mindfulness, we can transform our approach to stress and enhance our overall well-being. The strategies and practices outlined in this chapter provide a foundation for building a resilient, positive, and mindful mindset that can help navigate life's challenges with greater ease and confidence.

Resources

1. **Books:**

   - "Mindset: The New Psychology of Success" by Carol S. Dweck

   - "The Resilience Factor: 7 Keys to Finding Your Inner Strength and Overcoming Life's Hurdles" by Karen Reivich and Andrew Shatté

   - "The Power of Positive Thinking" by Norman Vincent Peale

   - "The Gratitude Diaries: How a Year Looking on the Bright Side Can Transform Your Life" by Janice Kaplan

2. **Websites:**

- Positive Psychology Center (www.ppc.sas.upenn.edu)

- Greater Good Science Center (www.greatergood.berkeley.edu)

- Mindful (www.mindful.org)

3. **Apps:**

- Headspace (mindfulness and meditation)

- Calm (meditation and relaxation)

- Happify (positive psychology and well-being)

4. **Articles:**

- "How to Cultivate Gratitude" (Harvard Health Publishing)

- "Building Resilience" (American Psychological Association)

- "The Benefits of Mindfulness" (Mayo Clinic)

By integrating these insights and practices into daily life, individuals can create a robust and positive mindset that not only reduces stress but also enhances overall quality of life.

CHAPTER 3

PHYSICAL STRATEGIES FOR STRESS MANAGEMENT

"Take care of your body. It's the only place you have to live." —Jim Rohn

Introduction

The body and mind are deeply interconnected, and taking care of our physical health is essential for managing stress effectively. This chapter explores various physical strategies for stress management, including exercise and movement, nutrition and diet, sleep and relaxation, and breathing exercises. These approaches not only help in reducing stress but also enhance overall well-being, making them integral parts of a healthy lifestyle.

Exercise and Movement: The Role of Physical Activity in Reducing Stress

The Science Behind Exercise and Stress Relief

Regular physical activity is one of the most effective ways to combat stress. Exercise increases the production of endorphins, the brain's feel-good neurotransmitters, and reduces levels of the body's stress hormones, such as adrenaline and cortisol. Engaging in physical activity also improves sleep, which can be negatively affected by stress, anxiety, and depression.

Types of Exercise for Stress Relief

1. **Aerobic Exercise:** Activities like running, swimming, cycling, and brisk walking can significantly reduce stress. Aerobic exercises increase heart rate and oxygen intake, promoting cardiovascular health and releasing endorphins, which enhance mood.

2. **Strength Training:** Lifting weights or engaging in resistance training can help reduce anxiety and improve mental health. Strength training provides a sense of accomplishment and can increase self-esteem and resilience.

3. **Yoga:** Combining physical postures, breathing exercises, and meditation, yoga is a powerful practice for stress reduction. It helps improve flexibility, strength, and mental clarity while promoting relaxation and mindfulness.

4. **Tai Chi:** This gentle form of martial arts focuses on slow, deliberate movements and deep breathing. Tai Chi reduces stress, improves balance, and enhances overall well-being.

5. **Dancing:** Engaging in dance can be a fun and effective way to relieve stress. Dancing not only provides physical exercise but also allows for self-expression and social interaction, which can be beneficial for mental health.

Incorporating Exercise into Daily Life

Finding time for regular physical activity can be challenging, but incorporating small changes into daily routines can make a significant difference. Simple strategies include taking the stairs instead of the elevator, walking or biking to work, participating in group sports or classes, and scheduling regular workout sessions as part of a daily routine.

Nutrition and Diet: Foods That Help and Hinder Stress Management

The Connection Between Diet and Stress

What we eat can have a profound impact on how we feel. A balanced diet can help stabilize mood, improve energy levels, and enhance overall mental health, while poor nutrition can contribute to stress and anxiety. Understanding the role of nutrition in stress management is crucial for maintaining both physical and mental well-being.

Foods That Help Manage Stress

1. **Whole Grains:** Foods like oatmeal, brown rice, and whole wheat bread help regulate blood sugar levels and promote the release of serotonin, a neurotransmitter that improves mood and relaxation.

2. **Fruits and Vegetables:** Rich in vitamins, minerals, and antioxidants, fruits and vegetables support the immune system and reduce oxidative stress. Leafy greens, berries, and citrus fruits are particularly beneficial.

3. **Lean Proteins:** Sources of lean protein, such as chicken, turkey, fish, beans, and legumes, provide amino acids necessary for the production of neurotransmitters that

regulate mood.

4. **Nuts and Seeds:** Almonds, walnuts, flaxseeds, and chia seeds are rich in omega-3 fatty acids, which have been shown to reduce inflammation and promote brain health.

5. **Fermented Foods:** Yogurt, kefir, sauerkraut, and kimchi contain probiotics that support gut health and have been linked to improved mood and reduced anxiety.

6. **Herbal Teas:** Chamomile, lavender, and green tea can have calming effects and help reduce stress.

Foods That Hinder Stress Management

1. **Sugary Foods and Drinks:** High sugar intake can lead to energy crashes and mood swings. It can also increase the risk of developing chronic stress-related conditions.

2. **Caffeine:** While moderate caffeine consumption can improve focus and energy, excessive intake can lead to increased anxiety, jitteriness, and disrupted sleep.

3. **Alcohol:** Alcohol can initially have a relaxing effect, but excessive consumption can increase stress and anxiety levels and disrupt sleep patterns.

4. **Processed Foods:** Foods high in refined sugars, unhealthy fats, and additives can contribute to inflammation

and negatively affect mood and energy levels.

Tips for a Stress-Reducing Diet

1. **Plan Balanced Meals:** Ensure each meal includes a balance of lean proteins, healthy fats, and complex carbohydrates to maintain stable energy levels throughout the day.

2. **Stay Hydrated:** Drinking plenty of water helps maintain physical and mental functions. Dehydration can increase stress levels and reduce cognitive performance.

3. **Mindful Eating:** Pay attention to what you eat and savor each bite. Mindful eating can reduce overeating and improve digestion and satisfaction with meals.

Sleep and Relaxation: Importance of Quality Sleep and Techniques to Improve It

The Role of Sleep in Stress Management

Quality sleep is essential for emotional and physical health. During sleep, the body repairs itself, consolidates memories, and processes emotions. Lack of sleep can increase stress levels, impair cognitive function, and negatively affect mood and overall health.

Strategies to Improve Sleep Quality

1. **Establish a Sleep Routine:** Going to bed and waking up at the same time every day helps regulate the body's internal clock. Consistency is key to developing healthy sleep patterns.

2. **Create a Relaxing Sleep Environment:** A comfortable, quiet, and dark bedroom can promote better sleep. Investing in a good mattress and blackout curtains, and keeping the room cool, can improve sleep quality.

3. **Limit Screen Time:** Exposure to blue light from phones, tablets, and computers can interfere with the production of melatonin, a hormone that regulates sleep. Avoid screens at least an hour before bedtime.

4. **Avoid Stimulants:** Caffeine, nicotine, and heavy meals can disrupt sleep. Limiting these substances in the hours leading up to bedtime can improve sleep quality.

5. **Practice Relaxation Techniques:** Techniques such as reading, taking a warm bath, or listening to calming music before bed can signal to the body that it is time to unwind and prepare for sleep.

Breathing Exercises: Simple and Effective Breathing Techniques for Immediate Stress Relief

The Power of Breath

Breathing exercises are a simple yet powerful tool for managing stress. Controlled breathing can activate the parasympathetic nervous system, which helps calm the body and mind, reduce anxiety, and improve focus and relaxation.

Effective Breathing Techniques

1. **Deep Breathing:** Also known as diaphragmatic or belly breathing, this technique involves inhaling deeply through the nose, allowing the abdomen to expand, and then exhaling slowly through the mouth. This type of breathing promotes relaxation and reduces stress.

2. **4-7-8 Breathing:** This technique involves inhaling through the nose for a count of four, holding the breath for a count of seven, and exhaling slowly through the mouth for a count of eight. It can help reduce anxiety and promote a state of calm.

3. **Box Breathing:** Also known as square breathing, this technique involves inhaling for a count of four, holding the breath for a count of four, exhaling for a count of

four, and holding the breath again for a count of four. Box breathing can help improve focus and reduce stress.

4. **Alternate Nostril Breathing:** This technique involves closing one nostril and inhaling through the other, then closing the other nostril and exhaling through the first. Alternate nostril breathing can balance the body's energy and promote relaxation.

5. **Progressive Muscle Relaxation:** This technique combines deep breathing with tensing and relaxing different muscle groups. It can help reduce physical tension and promote a sense of relaxation.

Conclusion

Incorporating physical strategies into daily routines can significantly reduce stress and improve overall well-being. Exercise and movement, proper nutrition and diet, quality sleep, and breathing exercises are powerful tools for managing stress effectively. By understanding and implementing these strategies, individuals can enhance their physical and mental health, leading to a more balanced and fulfilling life.

Resources

1. **Books:**

- "Spark: The Revolutionary New Science of Exercise and the Brain" by John J. Ratey

- "The Sleep Solution: Why Your Sleep is Broken and How to Fix It" by W. Chris Winter

- "The Mind-Gut Connection" by Emeran Mayer

2. **Websites:**

- American Council on Exercise (www.acefitness.org)

- National Sleep Foundation (www.sleepfoundation.org)

- Academy of Nutrition and Dietetics (www.eatright.org)

3. **Apps:**

- MyFitnessPal (nutrition and exercise tracking)

- Sleep Cycle (sleep tracking)

- Breethe (meditation and breathing exercises)

4. **Articles:**

- "Exercise and Stress: Get Moving to Manage Stress" (Mayo Clinic)

- "Nutrition and Stress" (Harvard Health Publishing)

- "The Importance of Sleep for Health" (National Institutes of Health)

By integrating these physical strategies into daily life, individuals can effectively manage stress and enhance their overall health and well-being.

CHAPTER 4

EMOTIONAL AND SOCIAL STRATEGIES

"Emotional intelligence is not the opposite of intelligence, it is not the triumph of heart over head – it is the unique intersection of both." — *David Caruso*

Introduction

E motional and social strategies are crucial in managing stress effectively. While physical health is essential, our emotional well-being and the quality of our relationships significantly influence how we cope with stress. This chapter delves into understanding and managing emotions, building strong relationships, effective communication techniques, and the benefits of therapy and counseling. By enhancing emotional intelligence and leveraging social support, we can create a more resilient and balanced approach to stress management.

Emotional Intelligence: Understanding and Managing Emotions

What is Emotional Intelligence?

Emotional intelligence (EI) is the ability to recognize, understand, and manage our own emotions, as well as the emotions of others. It involves four key components: self-awareness, self-regulation, social awareness, and relationship management.

Components of Emotional Intelligence

1. **Self-Awareness:** The ability to recognize and understand our own emotions. Self-aware individuals can accurately assess their strengths and weaknesses, leading to better decision-making and stress management.

2. **Self-Regulation:** The ability to control or redirect disruptive emotions and impulses. Self-regulation helps individuals stay calm and composed under pressure, reducing the likelihood of stress-related reactions.

3. **Social Awareness:** The ability to understand the emotions and needs of others. This includes empathy, which allows individuals to connect with others and build

stronger relationships.

4. **Relationship Management:** The ability to develop and maintain healthy relationships through effective communication, conflict resolution, and teamwork.

Improving Emotional Intelligence

1. **Mindfulness Practices:** Techniques such as meditation and journaling can increase self-awareness and help individuals become more attuned to their emotions.

2. **Emotional Regulation Techniques:** Strategies such as deep breathing, cognitive reframing, and positive self-talk can help manage intense emotions and reduce stress.

3. **Empathy Development:** Practicing active listening and putting oneself in others' shoes can enhance empathy and social awareness.

4. **Social Skills Training:** Learning effective communication, conflict resolution, and teamwork skills can improve relationship management and reduce interpersonal stress.

Building Strong Relationships: The Role of Social Support in Stress Management

Importance of Social Support

Strong social support networks are vital for stress management. Positive relationships provide emotional comfort, practical assistance, and a sense of belonging, all of which can buffer against the negative effects of stress.

Types of Social Support

1. **Emotional Support:** This involves expressions of empathy, love, trust, and care. Emotional support can come from friends, family, partners, or support groups.

2. **Instrumental Support:** Practical help, such as financial assistance, childcare, or help with daily tasks, can alleviate stress by reducing the burden of responsibilities.

3. **Informational Support:** Providing advice, information, and feedback can help individuals navigate stressful situations more effectively.

4. **Appraisal Support:** This involves affirmation and constructive feedback that help individuals evaluate and understand their situations better.

Building and Maintaining Strong Relationships

1. **Invest Time and Effort:** Regularly spending time with

loved ones and engaging in shared activities strengthens bonds and enhances social support.

2. **Communicate Openly:** Honest and open communication fosters trust and understanding in relationships. Expressing feelings and concerns can prevent misunderstandings and conflicts.

3. **Be Supportive:** Offering help, listening actively, and showing empathy can strengthen relationships and encourage reciprocity.

4. **Join Social Groups:** Participating in community groups, clubs, or activities that interest you can expand your social network and provide additional support.

Effective Communication: Techniques for Expressing Needs and Setting Boundaries

Importance of Effective Communication

Effective communication is crucial for managing stress in relationships. It helps in expressing needs, setting boundaries, and resolving conflicts, thereby reducing interpersonal stress and enhancing relationship quality.

Techniques for Effective Communication

1. **Active Listening:** Paying full attention to the speaker, showing empathy, and responding appropriately can foster understanding and reduce misunderstandings.

2. **Assertive Communication:** Expressing thoughts, feelings, and needs clearly and respectfully, without being aggressive or passive, helps in setting boundaries and preventing resentment.

3. **Nonverbal Communication:** Being aware of body language, facial expressions, and tone of voice can enhance communication and convey empathy and understanding.

4. **"I" Statements:** Using "I" statements (e.g., "I feel," "I need") instead of "you" statements can reduce defensiveness and promote constructive dialogue.

5. **Conflict Resolution Skills:** Learning to manage and resolve conflicts through negotiation, compromise, and problem-solving can reduce stress and strengthen relationships.

Setting Boundaries

1. **Identify Your Needs:** Understanding your own needs and limits is the first step in setting healthy boundaries.

2. **Communicate Clearly:** Clearly and respectfully communicate your boundaries to others. Be firm but polite in expressing what is acceptable and what is not.

3. **Be Consistent:** Consistency in enforcing boundaries is crucial for maintaining them. Stand by your boundaries even if it is uncomfortable.

4. **Respect Others' Boundaries:** Just as you set your boundaries, respect the boundaries set by others. This mutual respect fosters healthier relationships.

Therapeutic Approaches: Benefits of Therapy and Counseling

Understanding Therapy and Counseling

Therapy and counseling provide professional support for managing stress, improving emotional health, and developing coping strategies. Different therapeutic approaches can address various aspects of stress and emotional well-being.

Types of Therapy

1. **Cognitive Behavioral Therapy (CBT):** CBT focuses on identifying and changing negative thought patterns and behaviors. It is effective in managing stress, anxiety, and depression by promoting healthier ways of thinking

and coping.

2. **Mindfulness-Based Stress Reduction (MBSR):** MBSR combines mindfulness practices with stress reduction techniques. It helps individuals become more aware of their thoughts and emotions, reducing stress and improving overall well-being.

3. **Acceptance and Commitment Therapy (ACT):** ACT encourages acceptance of thoughts and feelings rather than fighting them. It helps individuals commit to actions that align with their values, despite emotional discomfort.

4. **Interpersonal Therapy (IPT):** IPT focuses on improving interpersonal relationships and communication patterns. It is effective in reducing stress related to relationship conflicts and social interactions.

5. **Dialectical Behavior Therapy (DBT):** DBT combines cognitive-behavioral techniques with mindfulness practices. It is particularly effective for managing intense emotions and improving emotional regulation.

Benefits of Therapy and Counseling

1. **Emotional Support:** Therapy provides a safe and non-judgmental space to explore emotions and experiences, offering emotional support and validation.

2. **Stress Reduction:** Therapeutic techniques help individuals develop effective coping strategies for managing stress and reducing its impact on daily life.

3. **Improved Relationships:** Therapy can enhance communication skills, resolve conflicts, and improve relationship quality, reducing interpersonal stress.

4. **Increased Self-Awareness:** Therapy promotes self-awareness and insight, helping individuals understand their emotions, behaviors, and thought patterns.

5. **Enhanced Coping Skills:** Therapy equips individuals with practical tools and techniques for managing stress, anxiety, and other emotional challenges.

Conclusion

Emotional and social strategies are essential for effective stress management. By understanding and managing emotions, building strong relationships, practicing effective communication, and seeking therapeutic support, individuals can enhance their resilience and overall well-being. These strategies provide a comprehensive approach to managing stress, promoting emotional health, and fostering meaningful connections with others.

Resources

1. **Books:**

   - "Emotional Intelligence: Why It Can Matter More Than IQ" by Daniel Goleman

   - "Nonviolent Communication: A Language of Life" by Marshall B. Rosenberg

   - "The Body Keeps the Score: Brain, Mind, and Body in the Healing of Trauma" by Bessel van der Kolk

2. **Websites:**

   - The Gottman Institute (www.gottman.com)

   - American Psychological Association (www.apa.org)

   - National Institute of Mental Health (www.nimh.nih.gov)

3. **Apps:**

   - Headspace (meditation and mindfulness)

   - BetterHelp (online therapy)

   - Talkspace (online therapy)

4. **Articles:**

- ○ "The Importance of Emotional Intelligence in the Workplace" (Harvard Business Review)

- ○ "Building Stronger Relationships" (Psychology Today)

- ○ "Effective Communication: Improving Your Social Skills" (Mayo Clinic)

By integrating these emotional and social strategies into daily life, individuals can manage stress more effectively, enhance their emotional health, and build stronger, more supportive relationships.

Chapter 5

TIME MANAGEMENT AND PRODUCTIVITY

"Time management is life management." — Robin Sharma

Introduction

In today's fast-paced world, managing time effectively is crucial for maintaining productivity and reducing stress. This chapter explores the importance of prioritizing and planning, avoiding burnout, achieving work-life balance, and overcoming procrastination and perfectionism. By mastering these time management and productivity techniques, you can enhance your efficiency, well-being, and overall quality of life.

Prioritizing and Planning: Techniques for Effective Time Management

The Importance of Prioritization

Effective time management begins with prioritization. Understanding what tasks are most important and tackling them first can significantly improve productivity.

Techniques for Prioritization

1. **Eisenhower Matrix:** This technique involves categorizing tasks into four quadrants based on urgency and importance:

   - Urgent and important

   - Important but not urgent

   - Urgent but not important

   - Neither urgent nor important

2. **ABC Method:** This method involves labeling tasks as A, B, or C based on their priority. 'A' tasks are the highest priority, 'B' tasks are medium priority, and 'C' tasks are low priority.

3. **80/20 Rule (Pareto Principle):** Focus on the 20% of

tasks that yield 80% of the results. Identifying and prioritizing these high-impact tasks can greatly enhance productivity.

Planning Strategies

1. **Daily To-Do Lists:** Creating a daily list of tasks helps organize your day and ensure that important tasks are not overlooked.

2. **Time Blocking:** This involves dedicating specific blocks of time to different tasks or activities. It helps to structure your day and allocate sufficient time for important tasks.

3. **Goal Setting:** Setting clear, achievable goals provides direction and motivation. Break down long-term goals into smaller, manageable tasks to track progress effectively.

Avoiding Burnout: Recognizing the Signs and Taking Preventive Measures

Understanding Burnout

Burnout is a state of physical, emotional, and mental exhaustion caused by prolonged stress. It can significantly impact productivity and well-being.

Signs of Burnout

1. **Chronic Fatigue:** Feeling constantly tired and drained, even after adequate rest.

2. **Decreased Performance:** Struggling to complete tasks and experiencing a decline in productivity.

3. **Emotional Exhaustion:** Feeling overwhelmed, detached, or emotionally drained.

4. **Physical Symptoms:** Experiencing headaches, muscle pain, or other stress-related physical issues.

Preventive Measures

1. **Regular Breaks:** Taking short, frequent breaks during work can prevent fatigue and maintain productivity.

2. **Healthy Lifestyle:** Maintaining a balanced diet, regular exercise, and adequate sleep helps manage stress and prevent burnout.

3. **Stress Management Techniques:** Practices such as mindfulness, meditation, and deep breathing can reduce stress levels.

4. **Set Boundaries:** Establishing clear boundaries between work and personal life helps to prevent overwork and

maintain a healthy balance.

Work-Life Balance: Strategies to Balance Professional and Personal Life

Importance of Work-Life Balance

Achieving a healthy work-life balance is essential for maintaining overall well-being and productivity. It helps to prevent burnout and ensures that personal and professional life are in harmony.

Strategies for Work-Life Balance

1. **Set Priorities:** Identify and prioritize what is most important in both your professional and personal life.

2. **Create a Schedule:** Develop a daily or weekly schedule that allocates time for work, family, leisure, and self-care.

3. **Learn to Say No:** Avoid overcommitting by recognizing your limits and saying no to additional tasks or responsibilities when necessary.

4. **Delegate Tasks:** Share responsibilities at work and home to reduce your workload and stress.

5. **Unplug:** Disconnect from work-related technology during personal time to ensure quality rest and leisure.

Procrastination and Perfectionism: Overcoming Common Productivity Barriers

Understanding Procrastination

Procrastination is the act of delaying tasks, often resulting in last-minute rushes and increased stress. It is a common barrier to productivity.

Causes of Procrastination

1. **Fear of Failure:** Avoiding tasks due to fear of making mistakes or failing.

2. **Lack of Motivation:** Struggling to find interest or motivation to start a task.

3. **Perfectionism:** Delaying tasks due to unrealistic standards and the desire for everything to be perfect.

Techniques to Overcome Procrastination

1. **Break Tasks into Smaller Steps:** Breaking down large tasks into smaller, manageable steps makes them less daunting and easier to start.

2. **Set Deadlines:** Establishing specific deadlines for tasks creates a sense of urgency and helps to overcome procras-

tination.

3. **Use the Pomodoro Technique:** This involves working for 25 minutes followed by a 5-minute break, which can improve focus and productivity.

4. **Eliminate Distractions:** Identify and remove potential distractions to create a conducive work environment.

Understanding Perfectionism

Perfectionism involves setting excessively high standards and striving for flawlessness, which can hinder productivity and increase stress.

Overcoming Perfectionism

1. **Set Realistic Goals:** Establish achievable and realistic goals instead of striving for perfection.

2. **Focus on Progress, Not Perfection:** Emphasize progress and improvement rather than flawless outcomes.

3. **Accept Mistakes:** Recognize that mistakes are part of the learning process and an opportunity for growth.

4. **Practice Self-Compassion:** Be kind to yourself and acknowledge your efforts and achievements.

Conclusion

Effective time management and productivity are vital for reducing stress and enhancing overall well-being. By prioritizing and planning tasks, avoiding burnout, achieving work-life balance, and overcoming procrastination and perfectionism, you can optimize your productivity and lead a more balanced and fulfilling life. These strategies not only improve efficiency but also promote a healthier and more sustainable approach to managing time and stress.

Resources

1. **Books:**

   - "Getting Things Done: The Art of Stress-Free Productivity" by David Allen

   - "The 7 Habits of Highly Effective People" by Stephen R. Covey

   - "Atomic Habits: An Easy & Proven Way to Build Good Habits & Break Bad Ones" by James Clear

2. **Websites:**

   - MindTools (www.mindtools.com)

   - American Psychological Association (www.apa.org)

- Harvard Business Review (hbr.org)

3. **Apps:**

- Todoist (task management)

- Trello (project management)

- Focus@Will (productivity music)

4. **Articles:**

- "How to Prioritize When Everything Feels Important" (Harvard Business Review)

- "10 Strategies for Avoiding Burnout" (Psychology Today)

- "Achieving Work-Life Balance" (Mayo Clinic)

By implementing these time management and productivity techniques, you can effectively manage stress, improve efficiency, and achieve a healthier work-life balance. These strategies provide a comprehensive approach to enhancing productivity and well-being, empowering you to make the most of your time and lead a more fulfilling life.

CHAPTER 6

LONG-TERM STRATEGIES FOR STRESS MASTERY

*"Stress is not what happens to us. It's our response
to what happens. And response is something we can
choose." — Maureen Killoran*

Introduction

Mastering stress requires more than short-term fixes; it involves developing long-term strategies that become an integral part of daily life. This chapter explores how to create a stress-resilient lifestyle, the importance of hobbies and leisure activities, continuous learning and growth, and personal growth and self-care. By incorporating these elements into your life, you can build a robust foundation for managing stress and enhancing overall well-being.

Creating a Stress-Resilient Lifestyle: Integrating Stress Management into Daily Life

Building Resilience

Resilience is the ability to bounce back from adversity. A stress-resilient lifestyle involves habits and practices that strengthen your capacity to handle stress.

Key Components of a Stress-Resilient Lifestyle

1. **Healthy Habits:** Maintaining a balanced diet, regular exercise, and adequate sleep are fundamental to resilience. These habits enhance physical health, which in turn supports mental and emotional well-being.

2. **Mindfulness and Relaxation:** Incorporating mindfulness practices such as meditation, deep breathing, and yoga can help reduce stress and improve emotional regulation.

3. **Positive Relationships:** Building and maintaining supportive relationships provide emotional support and a sense of belonging, which are crucial for resilience.

4. **Work-Life Balance:** Striking a balance between professional and personal life prevents burnout and ensures time for relaxation and enjoyment.

5. **Time Management:** Effective time management techniques, such as prioritizing tasks and avoiding procrastination, can reduce stress and enhance productivity.

Strategies for Integration

1. **Routine Establishment:** Create daily routines that include time for exercise, relaxation, and social interaction. Consistent routines can provide stability and reduce stress.

2. **Setting Boundaries:** Establish clear boundaries between work and personal life to ensure time for rest and leisure.

3. **Stress Reduction Techniques:** Regularly practice stress reduction techniques such as mindfulness, deep breathing, and progressive muscle relaxation.

4. **Positive Mindset:** Cultivate a positive mindset by focusing on gratitude, practicing positive self-talk, and reframing negative thoughts.

Hobbies and Leisure Activities: Importance of Downtime and Fun

The Role of Hobbies

Engaging in hobbies and leisure activities is essential for reducing stress and enhancing overall well-being. These activities provide a break from daily responsibilities and offer opportunities for enjoyment and creativity.

Benefits of Hobbies

1. **Stress Reduction:** Hobbies can provide a mental break and help shift focus away from stressors, leading to relaxation and reduced anxiety.

2. **Improved Mood:** Engaging in enjoyable activities releases endorphins, which can improve mood and overall happiness.

3. **Social Interaction:** Many hobbies involve social interaction, which can enhance relationships and provide emotional support.

4. **Skill Development:** Hobbies often involve learning new skills, which can boost confidence and provide a sense of accomplishment.

Incorporating Hobbies into Daily Life

1. **Make Time for Fun:** Schedule regular time for hobbies and leisure activities, just as you would for work or other responsibilities.

2. **Explore New Interests:** Try new activities to discover what you enjoy and what helps you relax.

3. **Join Clubs or Groups:** Participate in clubs or groups related to your hobbies to meet like-minded people and enhance social interaction.

4. **Balance Activities:** Ensure a balance between solitary and social activities to meet your personal needs and preferences.

Continuous Learning and Growth: Staying Informed and Adapting to Change

Importance of Continuous Learning

Lifelong learning is crucial for personal growth and adaptability. Staying informed and continuously developing new skills can help manage stress and navigate life's challenges more effectively.

Benefits of Continuous Learning

1. **Enhanced Adaptability:** Learning new skills and knowledge can improve your ability to adapt to changes and overcome obstacles.

2. **Cognitive Stimulation:** Engaging in learning activities stimulates the brain and can enhance cognitive function and mental acuity.

3. **Increased Confidence:** Acquiring new knowledge and skills can boost self-confidence and self-efficacy.

4. **Personal Fulfillment:** Continuous learning provides a sense of accomplishment and can lead to personal fulfillment and growth.

Strategies for Continuous Learning

1. **Set Learning Goals:** Identify areas of interest or skills you want to develop and set specific learning goals.

2. **Utilize Resources:** Take advantage of resources such as books, online courses, workshops, and seminars to enhance your knowledge and skills.

3. **Stay Curious:** Maintain a curious mindset and seek opportunities to learn from everyday experiences and interactions.

4. **Apply Knowledge:** Apply what you learn in practical ways to reinforce learning and enhance its relevance to your life.

Personal Growth and Self-Care: Developing a Personalized Stress Management Plan

Personal Growth

Personal growth involves striving to become the best version of yourself. It includes self-awareness, self-improvement, and the pursuit of meaningful goals.

Components of Personal Growth

1. **Self-Reflection:** Regularly reflect on your values, goals, and experiences to gain insights into your personal growth journey.

2. **Goal Setting:** Set meaningful and achievable goals that align with your values and aspirations.

3. **Emotional Intelligence:** Develop emotional intelligence skills to enhance self-awareness, self-regulation, and interpersonal relationships.

4. **Resilience Building:** Foster resilience through practices such as mindfulness, positive self-talk, and stress manage-

ment techniques.

Self-Care

Self-care involves taking deliberate actions to care for your physical, emotional, and mental well-being. It is essential for maintaining overall health and managing stress.

Elements of Self-Care

1. **Physical Self-Care:** Maintain a balanced diet, regular exercise, and adequate sleep to support physical health.

2. **Emotional Self-Care:** Engage in activities that promote emotional well-being, such as mindfulness, journaling, and spending time with loved ones.

3. **Mental Self-Care:** Stimulate your mind through continuous learning, reading, and engaging in creative activities.

4. **Social Self-Care:** Foster positive relationships and seek social support when needed.

Developing a Personalized Stress Management Plan

1. **Assess Your Needs:** Identify your stressors, strengths, and areas for improvement.

2. **Set Goals:** Establish specific, achievable goals for manag-

ing stress and enhancing well-being.

3. **Create a Routine:** Develop a daily routine that incorporates self-care activities, stress reduction techniques, and time for hobbies and relaxation.

4. **Seek Support:** Reach out to friends, family, or professionals for support and guidance in your stress management journey.

5. **Monitor Progress:** Regularly review and adjust your stress management plan to ensure it meets your needs and goals.

Conclusion

Long-term strategies for stress mastery involve creating a stress-resilient lifestyle, incorporating hobbies and leisure activities, embracing continuous learning and growth, and prioritizing personal growth and self-care. By integrating these elements into daily life, you can build a strong foundation for managing stress and enhancing overall well-being. These strategies provide a holistic approach to stress management, empowering you to lead a more balanced, fulfilling, and resilient life.

Resources

1. **Books:**

- "The Stress-Proof Brain: Master Your Emotional Response to Stress Using Mindfulness and Neuroplasticity" by Melanie Greenberg

- "Resilient: How to Grow an Unshakable Core of Calm, Strength, and Happiness" by Rick Hanson

- "The How of Happiness: A New Approach to Getting the Life You Want" by Sonja Lyubomirsky

2. **Websites:**

- American Psychological Association (www.apa.org)

- Mindful (www.mindful.org)

- Psychology Today (www.psychologytoday.com)

3. **Apps:**

- Calm (meditation and relaxation)

- Headspace (mindfulness and meditation)

- Coursera (online learning)

4. **Articles:**

- "Building Resilience" (Harvard Business Review)

- "The Importance of Hobbies for Stress Relief" (Psychology Today)

- "Continuous Learning for Personal Growth" (Forbes)

By adopting these long-term strategies for stress mastery, you can cultivate resilience, enhance your well-being, and lead a more balanced and fulfilling life. Integrating these practices into your daily routine will empower you to manage stress effectively and thrive in all aspects of life.

CONCLUSION

"The greatest weapon against stress is our ability to choose one thought over another." — William James

Recap of Key Points: Summary of the Main Strategies Discussed

Understanding Stress

1. **Definition and Types of Stress:** Stress can be acute, chronic, or eustress. Understanding these types helps in identifying the nature of stress experienced.

2. **Physiology of Stress:** Stress affects the body and mind through various physiological responses, including the activation of the fight-or-flight response.

3. **Identifying Stressors:** Common sources of stress in-

clude work, relationships, financial concerns, and health issues.

4. **Self-Assessment:** Tools such as stress inventories and self-reflection techniques help in identifying personal stress levels and triggers.

Mindset and Attitude

1. **Power of Perspective:** How we perceive stress significantly influences our experience and response to it. Cultivating a positive mindset can mitigate the impact of stress.

2. **Developing Resilience:** Building mental toughness involves practices such as mindfulness, gratitude, and positive self-talk.

3. **Positive Thinking:** Techniques to cultivate a positive outlook include affirmations, visualization, and cognitive restructuring.

4. **Gratitude and Mindfulness:** Regularly practicing gratitude and mindfulness shifts focus away from stressors and promotes emotional well-being.

Physical Strategies for Stress Management

1. **Exercise and Movement:** Regular physical activity reduces stress hormones and boosts endorphins, enhancing

mood and resilience.

2. **Nutrition and Diet:** Consuming a balanced diet rich in nutrients supports overall health and helps manage stress.

3. **Sleep and Relaxation:** Quality sleep is crucial for stress recovery. Techniques such as sleep hygiene and relaxation exercises improve sleep quality.

4. **Breathing Exercises:** Simple breathing techniques, such as deep breathing and progressive muscle relaxation, provide immediate stress relief.

Emotional and Social Strategies

1. **Emotional Intelligence:** Understanding and managing emotions is key to reducing stress and improving relationships.

2. **Building Strong Relationships:** Social support from family, friends, and colleagues provides emotional comfort and reduces stress.

3. **Effective Communication:** Expressing needs and setting boundaries through assertive communication prevents misunderstandings and conflicts.

4. **Therapeutic Approaches:** Therapy and counseling offer professional support for managing stress and emo-

tional challenges.

Time Management and Productivity

1. **Prioritizing and Planning:** Effective time management involves prioritizing tasks, setting goals, and using planning tools such as to-do lists and time blocking.

2. **Avoiding Burnout:** Recognizing signs of burnout and taking preventive measures such as regular breaks and healthy lifestyle choices.

3. **Work-Life Balance:** Balancing professional and personal life through strategies such as setting boundaries and delegating tasks.

4. **Procrastination and Perfectionism:** Overcoming productivity barriers by breaking tasks into smaller steps, setting realistic goals, and practicing self-compassion.

Long-Term Strategies for Stress Mastery

1. **Creating a Stress-Resilient Lifestyle:** Integrating healthy habits, mindfulness, and positive relationships into daily life.

2. **Hobbies and Leisure Activities:** Engaging in enjoyable activities provides relaxation and reduces stress.

3. **Continuous Learning and Growth:** Lifelong learning enhances adaptability and personal fulfillment.

4. **Personal Growth and Self-Care:** Developing a personalized stress management plan that includes self-reflection, goal setting, and self-care practices.

Encouragement: Final Words of Motivation and Empowerment

Managing stress is not a one-time effort but a continuous journey of growth and self-improvement. It requires dedication, self-awareness, and the willingness to adopt new habits and strategies. Remember that stress is a natural part of life, and learning to manage it effectively can lead to greater resilience, well-being, and happiness. You have the power to choose how you respond to stress and to implement the techniques that work best for you.

Believe in your ability to handle challenges and stay committed to your personal growth and well-being. Celebrate your progress, no matter how small, and be kind to yourself along the way. Stress management is an evolving process, and with consistent effort, you can master it and lead a balanced, fulfilling life.

Resources: Additional Reading, Tools, and Support for Ongoing Stress Mastery

Books

1. **"The Relaxation and Stress Reduction Workbook" by Martha Davis, Elizabeth Robbins Eshelman, and Matthew McKay:** A comprehensive guide with practical exercises for managing stress.

2. **"The Happiness Project" by Gretchen Rubin:** Insights and strategies for finding happiness and reducing stress through personal growth.

3. **"When the Body Says No: Exploring the Stress-Disease Connection" by Gabor Maté:** An exploration of how chronic stress impacts physical health and ways to address it.

Websites

1. **American Institute of Stress (www.stress.org):** Resources, articles, and tools for understanding and managing stress.

2. **Mindful (www.mindful.org):** Information on mindfulness practices, meditation guides, and stress reduction techniques.

3. **Psychology Today (www.psychologytoday.com)**: Articles and resources on stress management, mental health, and well-being.

Apps

1. **Calm:** Guided meditations, sleep stories, and relaxation exercises to reduce stress.

2. **Headspace:** Mindfulness and meditation app with courses on stress management and emotional well-being.

3. **Insight Timer:** Meditation app with a large library of guided meditations and relaxation music.

Support Groups

1. **Online Support Communities:** Join online forums and groups focused on stress management and mental health for peer support and shared experiences.

2. **Local Support Groups:** Look for local support groups or community centers that offer stress management workshops and meetings.

3. **Professional Counseling:** Consider seeking support from a licensed therapist or counselor for personalized guidance and support.

By utilizing these resources and continuing to practice the strategies discussed in this book, you can develop a robust approach to managing stress. Remember, the journey to mastering stress is ongoing, and every step you take brings you closer to a more balanced, fulfilling, and resilient life.

MAY I ASK YOU FOR A SMALL FAVOR?

I want to express my sincere gratitude for choosing to invest your time in reading this book. Your decision to explore this work among countless others means a lot to me.

I hope that within these pages, you've discovered actionable insights that can enhance your daily life. Your journey doesn't have to end here, though.

May I kindly request an additional 30 seconds of your valuable time?

Sharing your thoughts about the book through a review would be immensely appreciated. Your review serves as a beacon, guiding other readers to take a chance on my books. It's a small gesture that carries significant weight in the world of authors.

To submit your review effortlessly, please click on the link below. It will take you directly to the book's review page:

"The Stress Detox"

Alternatively, you can also find the "**Reviews Section**" of this book's page on Amazon.

Your review will require just a minute of your time but will make a monumental difference in helping me connect with a broader audience and I eagerly look forward to reading your review.

Once again, thank you for your unwavering support of my work.

DISCLAIMER

This book is for educational purposes only. Readers acknowledge that the author does not render legal, financial, medical, or professional advice. The content within this book has been derived from various sources. Please consult a licensed professional before attempting any techniques outlined in this book.

By reading this document, the reader agrees that under no circumstances is the author responsible for any direct or indirect losses incurred as a result of the use of the information contained within this document, including but not limited to errors, omissions, or inaccuracies.

Adherence to all applicable laws and regulations, including international, federal, state, and local governing professional licensing, business practices, advertising, and all other jurisdictions, is the sole responsibility of the purchaser or reader.

Neither the author nor the publisher assumes any responsibility or liability whatsoever on behalf of the purchaser or reader of these materials. Any perceived slight of any individual or organization is purely unintentional.

www.ingramcontent.com/pod-product-compliance
Lightning Source LLC
Chambersburg PA
CBHW050652250726
48662CB00002B/624